My Sweet Black
An Unruly Hymn

T. S. Holmes, III

Holmes, Theodore Sylvester, III
My Sweet Black, An Unruly Hymn

Summary: A collection of poetry, notes, and essays to celebrate and shed light on the Black experience.

http://www.teddythebrave.com

Published By:
BookBaby
7905 N Crescent Blvd.
Pennsauken, NJ 08110

Printed in the United States of America
Cover Illustration by Kendal D. Howard
Cover Photography by Brandon J. Brooks

First Paperback Edition, 2021
ISBN 978-1098385477
eBook ISBN 978-1098385484

I stood on the banks of the low country -there in the Gullah waters- and I washed. Somewhere in there were my great-great-great- grandmother's tears. Making me whole.

Set my feet on the ground anew. I walked into the wood to build me an altar on hallowed ground. I sang until the ancient magic loosened the soil and spiraled up from the ground. Wrapping me in fierce light.

Not a soul could hinder me as I took to the sky on holy embers . . . and on wings that only be worn by the righteous and the weary.

Flew away to meet my people-how wonderful they are. Standing face to face in the high holy heavens with image-bearing kin.

An image-bearing son.

Contents

Preface

I remember when Philando was murdered. I didn't leave my room for days. At the weeks end, I decided to go to a church service. I thought for sure that I'd find understanding and comfort there. I arrived in the thick of a pre-service prayer. The microphone was open to the lay members. A White man proceeded to pray, "And Lord, with all this craziness that's going on, help them to remember that at the end of the day, it's not about race because you don't see color. We all bleed red." All that this ailing Black man heard was a plea for the angry Black folks to stop whining. It was delivered in the same "what more do you want" attitude I had grown accustomed to when dealing with many other White male leaders be it in the workplace, schoolhouse, or anywhere- a blatant dismal.

I quickly turned around and started for the door. My stomach was turning as he worked to purge the sanctuary of my God-given rightfulness to stand there in my Blackness. I was undone with disgust at the subtle call for cultural assimilation. I was mortified as I glanced back at my own acquiescence from those past several years. I was smiley, subdued, agreeable and always trying to prove that I was worthy to all my White counterparts, seeking their approval.

When I allowed myself to break and be angry, pissed-off, sad, and grief-stricken, I found a well. It was overflowing with so much goodness. There was a newfound centeredness and a natural affinity to the sacred bond to my people. I realized I loved being Black and perhaps I'd had a subconscious fear of being rejected or harmed. And now, I never wanted to take it for granted. Others could and would take it for granted, but I must not. And so be it, I would not-ever again. My eyes were opened.

I began keeping a collection of songs and essays and poems that became a safe place for me to celebrate and honor my

Blackness. All the pain and mystery. All of the magic and wisdom. The richness. The power. The sweet-a syrupy sweet. The poignancy. The fury. The struggle and innovation. And so here we are, my first book of poetry with nothing but my Blackness to give and it is more than enough.

I have found that whenever I've lifted my voice for the sake of freedom, justice, or celebration, I have been written off as a threat. Whenever someone speaks of Black people as having wealth, intelligence, or love, it almost always becomes an impossible equation of a confrontation. Many people are not well with Black people and the affluence we carry. Some have even groomed, within their generations, the idea that Black people are built for blows and hardship and that we are eventually disposable. Some cannot believe that we are actual people-perhaps a subconscious knowing on their part, a fear that our worthiness might invalidate theirs. It becomes too big of an allowance in a colonialist society. Our very humanity then, becomes something to be feared and conquered all over again in brutish and unimaginable ways.

Unruly, the way we thrive in the sun. Unruly, the way we build and invent. The way we defend and protect! Unruly, the way we love, seek and appeal to Creator. Unruly, our rhythm and song. Unruly, this hair that stands tall- curls, strong. Fearless and flaring, these noses spread wide. We are undesired, but we are a self-loving people.

In the spirit of all my ancestors who now guide me in my personal rebellion, I offer up this first collection. An ode to us. A great juba! A prayer. A wail. A banner. A cloak for all the Black people who are constantly dismissed in apparent and unspoken places. My Sweet Black.

AN UNRULY HYMN

I light this fire
An untamed torch
In the spirit of all my ancestors
In a bold display of fragrant melody, I bury the dirge with a
hymn
A song for them who were burned and beat
I beat the drum over their posterity
We wake the dawn

We are closer to remembering how it was always supposed to
be
We been free
Stayed so long under latch and key
A hundred and a hundred and a hundred years later,
A nation implies it's normalcy-
Not me
I'm up now- I take my freedom standing up
I take my freedom un-cuffed
I am too free to be lulled by the system
I am too Africa to be discounted treasure

I am valuable forever

An untamed torch
Ablaze with the spirit of my ancestors
A contemporary nightmare
A fire unearthed
A new song, their song rebirthed
Crowned, enthroned, and seated at the right hand side of all of
them- **An Unruly Hymn**

The other children called him Kinky Bush. That was 'cause his hair was thick as a bale of hay and kinked like a lamb's wool. Everyday they found that boy and taunted him-his hair, his walk, and his skin. They bet money that his folks were uglier than him. They taunted him because he was different. They nagged him because he walked kingly- truth is, he appeared so kingly they didn't know what to do but keep on teasing him. They thought he was delusional. They thought he was sick. They thought he wasn't fit to be around the other kids.

All of this and Kinky Bush just laughed. He came to school smiling and left the same. He grew more intimidating by the day. Ever heard of laughing at something you fear? This boy was something to marvel. Though he was the butt of their jokes, he never misspoke. No matter how he was tarnished, no one could deny the strange sense of bigness the boy carried inside him. If you stared long enough, he seemed like he had wings. Like magic surrounded him. They felt when he was near and dreaded his very presence. After some time they stopped teasing him from the sidelines and started to askin' 'em questions.

"Say boy, don't you feel no hurt when harm come your way?" To which he laughed.

"It must be true that niggras don't feel nothing 'til you near 'bout kill em." He laughed heartily.

"Boy you better say something!" And the crowd of taunting kids fired up their assaults.

The boy stood up and said with the strength of a thousand voices, "My Blackness might as well be for gladness. I am protected by heavenly masses. Strong shoulders, swift fleets of Black angels. And they have been watching over me. They love me and they guide me. I laugh because I got something you can't see. An army of Love marches with me. And besides, I know that those who have mocked me will eat from

3

their own trees. I have plead mercy for you and for all this time, but I cannot stop it from happening now."

He started laughing and speaking in unfamiliar tongues. A few of the ringleaders tried to rev up the mocking again, but it failed. Some of the girls tried to go back to playing patty cake and house but it stalled. Teachers stepped out to see what was happening and they were stunned to muteness. Kinky Bush clapped his hands and beat the ground like a drum. He laughed and sang and ran around some. And then there was silence- an eerie damning silence- a silence that begged desperately for a second chance.

Kinky rose to his feet and began to walk away singing like nothing had happened. It seemed like he was floating away or perhaps flying. "Ain't afraid of no witchin' niggers!" Cried one of the other boys. Soon the teachers had all the children grab a bible and recite scriptures. They called the local pastor to come and pray. As he entered, he was met with a chorus of scriptures spoken by flustered youth.

"Fix your eyes on Jesus Children!" said the pastor. One of the children cried out, "but Kinky said Jesus is Black and what if Jesus is witchin' too?" The children started crying and panicking. It was a real show. The pastor grew angry and shouted out, " Ain't no nigger gonna tell me who my Lord is. Now I'll be damned if we gon' let this mangy tar baby spook us to death! The Lord is my shepherd. Say it with me, The Lord is my Shepherd!" They all began to repeat the phrase with a sort of false confidence. That night they took to their beds a tremblin'. Something was to come.

The next day, there was no trace of the school, the students, the pastor, or the very foundation on which the community stood. And down by the river over in a nearby city, the boy sat, kinked and bushy, saying "I got something you see." And he laughed more heartily than before.

4

I WILL NOT BE BLACK FOR YOU TODAY

> "Hey, do that thing you do!
> I'll pay, too!
> Talk that talk, walk that walk
> and shimmy for me baby.
> Sing! Sing!"

THE TUNES IN MY HEAD ARE MINE TODAY

won't be singing 'em for you
won't be no moving you to tears with the sad slave song
milking me like that- you know you wrong
gulp me down like a root beer float
lick me off your top lip
my sugar coursing through your body.
I am not your grandmother's hot 'n toddy

HEAL YOURSELF

will you stop at nothing to get the gold?
you mighty bold
give it back to Africa, everything you stole.
before you came boppin' up in here,
we were just kings and queens at home
but you couldn't just take the riches,
you had to taste the "soul"

I know, we cool
hip
better than what you heard,
something like you've never known
our sex, hair, hips, mind,
our heaping piles of magic
the music, the mystery, the rhythm, and the passion
the science, the psychology, astrology, mathematics
the way the butters sit on our skin
the way the verse flows from our lips

5

and iterates itself on the wind
so our young will always remember
they are Black!
and there is so much majesty wrapped up in that
and I do not know where you plan to find some

BUT YOU CANNOT HAVE NONE OF MINES

I see the way you appropriate to pass the time
clawing away at this sugary sweet
trying to replicate what you see in me
but I am not your supply man
I will not be Black for you today

YOUR PILAGING HAS FOUND YOU IN DIRECT
CONTEMPT WITH THE UNIVERSE

old lady sue was a sight to behold

Dark as night, eyes like gold-

a well of beauty.

She seemed like a homeland for many a man who came
traveling.

Spirit would bring human folk to her door-

lost ones, Black ones- who couldn't find their way home.

They come a walking in their sleep from miles around

and Old Lady Sue would rise-

no matter the hour- she would rise with

an oracle on her lips,

a song in her heart.

They would look into her eyes and she would draw them in

and that is when the great dance would begin

-a healing step

a return to the sacred ritual.

Children of Africa found themselves again and again in the
bosom of Old Lady Sue.

Nobody know'd how, but she knew what to do.

Now, when the need be met and all is home and all is one,

she'd send them off before the morning sun

to wake with no inklin' of what had been done-

7

just faith and trust and the strength to go on.

Some folk called her a witch.

Some folk bow at her grace.

I tell you they called her the devil and she continued her work anyway!

And them who preyed on her magical ways

-threatened by her charm-

they soon be brought home out the cold.

I tell you what, it's the strangest thing,

one touch from Lady Sue will have you dancing in your dreams.

Jookin' and bendin', swingin' and stompin'.

I stayed up and watched 'em- it was the holiest thing I'd ever seen,

people dancing in their sleep,

dancing back home

lest they forget.

WILD THING

wild thing

stay frayed around the **edges**

your **essence** makes **embers** fly

you make this earth **extra** special

you **wild thing**

THE VILLAGE

Shadow John

Saw this man
Black like night
S curled, gelled down, texturized
Walking in this summer heat
-like there was no tomorrow.
He boarded the bus and for a moment
. . . my Uncle John was back.

Angels on Black Streets

dedicated to the old gent on the bike, on the corner of York Street & Freemason

he crossed the street on his bike
it looked as if traffic stood still for him
he had on a fedora
his gaze was set on me like he was fixed on telling me
something
he nodded his head then said, "Peace Man, be safe out there."

I've seen him in many skins
he speaks to me like I'm his next of kin
"What up Black?"
"What's good witcha Nep?"
"Blessings my Brotha"
"What goin' on witcha Boss Man?"
"What da bidness is Big Man?"
"Yo, Kid!"
"Jah Bless!"
"How 'bout it young man?"
"Hey King!"

But today I needed Peace.
I will forever be grateful for the angels posted up on Black
streets.

luevern

every gray,
every wrinkle,
every sag and dimple
she is far beyond the rank of beautiful-
a marvel when all is considered.
all fifty years of marriage,
all ten children,
a green thumb that would make even martha tremble.
she stirs the pot and turns nothing into dinner.
she is anything but simple-
that's one of cleo's daughters.
her hug becomes a home in which your heart is made tender.
her skin, ethereal to the touch.
her song, a fury-
a tribute

13

Before There Was Anxiety

there was a time
when all you needed to prosper
was a seat on a stoop
a comb, hair grease
a cool cousin or a big sister
parting your scalp

and sometimes a pack of sunflower seeds
and a long walk around the neighborhood
-back when everything was love
and you didn't have to be misunderstood
a vibe

I liked when the teacher would
buy me something on ice-cream day
tasting the colors of my favorite action hero
with the bubble gum drop in the middle
Ms. Faye was a real one

there was a time when I could look to the sky
and take in it's energy
and just be
We really could learn a thing or two from
the way it used to be
'cause now, we just anxious

Ruth Lane

I got the chance to be a kid again on ruth lane
my time to recover
my time to reclaim
my body, my will, my space
playtime with my cousins

In this house, you eat what you want
you laugh hard
play cards
and you sleep when you're done
laugh at folks you know- especially each other
share your favorite memories and things you had to suffer
watch game shows with your auntie and uncle
and just be with one another

we sing in this house
commercial breaks is our time to get down
at night, you can barely hear a sound, except for the tv
and sunday? we be up for church
some weekends I would ask my uncle for a couple of bucks
and he always gave me ten or twenty
it was his way of showing love

ruth lane was one of the places I really started to grow
I reclaimed the right to my family and the right to name that
place home
We have exited the center we've loved and known
but there will always be kirby's comedy show
there will always be burned cd's and family sing-a-longs
there will always be run o' nines and sets of fo's
there will always be the time I called ruth lane my own

The Mother

an ode to Wendy "Doc" Coleman, PhD and all Mothers
who have found their children

I tiptoed into her office. I thought I wore my mask well. I tried not to grab the snacks so eagerly. I tucked them away and breathed a sigh of relief-"food for another day." I really thought I had skated away, unnoticed-except mamas know. And for years, she circled me with armloads of blessings. It was communion. She did it in the name of God and in the name of all mothers. She did it in the name of her mother and my mother. She gave me bread and love and drink that I may grow big and strong and always remember . . . The Mother.

Ms. Lee

my grandma preach about doubting thomas
my grandma sacred like dalai lamas
my grandma save me jet magazines
my grandma pray the devil out me

my grandma buy me snacks after church
my grandma sent us to the store to work
my grandma laid a smooth foundation
my grandma is a giving sensation

my grandma got peanut butter crackers and pocket change and
sweets
to this day, my grandma stay watching out for me
my grandma is, always was, and will forever be
vada, pastor, and especially ms. lee

The Watchmen

For Ms. Helen Young, Ms. Martistene Williams, Ms. Tia
Juana Malone, Curtis L. Williams, PhD, and all
Watchmen on my journey-before, now, and to come.
Thank you for bearing me up as village elders do.

they stood before the Council
he was coming
        -another one
they conceded to the invitation
he was coming
they didn't know when, but -he was their personal mission

they gathered at the welcoming gate
he didn't have a clue
they secretly watched over him for some time
        and then-a knock at their door
. . . it was him
the mild, genius, and incredibly wearied child
no place to go
they took him into their care

they encircled him
clothing him, feeding him
raising him up to leave
-for this was merely his fledgling home
he would soon be wanting to fly

they shielded him -armed, militant-
in his last days there
they taught him a way out and a way back
-though they knew, he would ultimately find his own
and they girded him in age-old secrets

in the circle, there was Light
a transference of sacred keys to unlock his magic
Black hands on Black shoulders
Black prayers and Black blessings
Black rods and Black thrashing-

provoking him to courage
he was ready

the unfoldment of his journey was commencing
he was in their care, but for a moment
but wherever he goes, he holds these Watchmen
who stood before the Council, vowing to love him

The Strength to Run On

I could have sworn today was Sunday by the way I waked not wanting to get out of the bed. But it was Saturday-and holy nonetheless. I hopped on my bike and slid down the streets to hit up the grocery store. Along the way, three Black aunties bid me safety. That's what we do in the village. We wish each other well. We speak. We offer emboldening sentiments. We name our young people as we would name our very children.

"Hey Baby, stay safe!"

"Hey Baby, you be safe!"

"Hey Punkin', stay hydrated and be safe!"

I was cheesing from ear to ear. "Yes Ma'am!" I replied to all, pedaling with a newfound energy. I knew I was supported. They sent me on with bits of their magic blistering behind me, bolstering me-holding up my hung down head. And it was in the authenticity of their presence that I found the strength to run on.

THE BLACK VOICE

It's the story that troubles me
the horror, the beauty
The God who allows it to run its course
the pain travailing down deep
the witness that won't let me sleep
until I confess that I have lived it. .
and God, (S)He bids me tell it

A Frustrated Artist on The Harvesting of "Blackness"

In an age where association and appropriation prevails, I find it incredibly wearying to constantly have my Blackness be a proven source of energy in spaces where I'm not welcomed. "What" I appear to be is totally allowable until "who" I am starts to occupy too much of those spaces. They want the *soulfulness*, they want the *cool*, but the Black person is not truly beloved. Black proves lucrative, but if you start mattering profoundly, you have to go . . . until the next consultation. "Black" is the sales pitch, but there are no seats for us at the table, though many of them have been built from our tree.

Quite plainly, I feel at times that we are being harvested for our Blackness. Equity is in question, yes? Or must we always be the Black opinion, the Black genius on the sidelines? Equity-centered conversations would mean acknowledging how we look at "power" in the Black person's hands. It would mean (for our White counterparts) acknowledging the unwillingness to share or relinquish a certain authority. This would mean breaking ties with a long-standing tradition of supremacy. It's everywhere. And as an artist, I have watched it for a long time. I've watched how it has morphed and seduced the White man, eventually fortifying the ignorance towards and the denial of Black and Brown truths.

Our Blackness is harvested for business and creative platforms. It is! How do we get that to change? We fight for spaces in which Black people can freely control their own narratives-even though there is always someone willing and convinced that they could help us tell it better. We stop allowing men to get the goods and run. Black people, cut the supply. We can build our own. And if we are attacked in our efforts- like in Tulsa- we can build again.

Call this a smack down on privilege if you feel so inclined, but if we are talking about unity and progression, then this IS about control because WE own our narratives. Do you pick every flower you see? Then sometimes it's okay to let what is, be. It behooves you (White collaborators, White industry, White enterprises) to listen to Black people instead of muzzling them while they tread YOUR corn. This is not the time to be practicing your great-great- grandfathers' antebellum schemes. It's time to pull up a few more seats at the table, before your exclusive empire fails you. Stop excluding Black bodies and Black experiences while calling in our energies and invaluableness. Stop harvesting our Blackness.

If Shakespeare was Black

If Shakespeare was Black

There might be little spoken of his life

His work? -masterful and unchanged

His wit? -striking and unmatched

But his fame? Hard to mutter

Hard to be discovered

unseen, Black

Sneakers

a street theory inspired by people I've met

one day I woke up-
and everybody was fighting
"I might fight you 'cause you lookin' at me"
"might be fighting 'cause we don't feel free"
I have lived to see the day that we are fighting over rations
while the White and elite stand back laughing
    -and the things they call us
they have us pinned right were they want us
in a quandary of circumstance

We have been fettered too long-
it's the fact that we were captive at all.
And now we are trying, but-
end up fighting each other while healing from the trauma.
and it don't come easy
we running out of ways to transmute this energy
we holding on to freedom but still have to fight the system
they gentrify, pipeline, so what do you expect, son?

I've heard them say we are the cause for our own hysteria-
I've heard them say BIPOC puts a damper on their America
but we are just trying to find our place-
    in a foreign land
trying to find our way home
trying to find where we can go-
to breathe
but they see through ill-fitted glasses
staring at a stereotype-
aiming at reasonable targets, considered reasonable game
instigating the ways we die and handle dying

    "let's casually kill these caricatures
    denying them their civil rights
    lets twist our faces when they fight back
    and pretend we are on their side
    let's lock them away in cages

until they starve for something tangible
something like . . . freedom
and when they ask for bread and water,
this is what we will feed 'em

toss them a taste of what it feels like
to have everything at your fingertips
to have- in every sense- a good life
toss them scraps, one of everything
and let them fight
they will be their own hindrance
they will be their own demise

and should they roar at us
when the scales fall off their eyes
we will charge them with the massacre
and build their cages high"

This is how the system has been playing victim
and letting itself win
slavery isn't general-it's really specific
specifically racist, classist, cotton pickin'
elite, inequitable, alive and kickin
and finding new ways to kill

one day I woke up-
and everybody was fighting
over colors
over lovers
-over whole human beings
over gas money
over territory
over food stamp cards
over paternity tests and cars
over clothes and broken tvs
. . . over sneakers
and something ain't right about it
seems induced
calculated
encouraged

Token

If I am your token
Then I am worth more than the richest of riches
or the riches of real kings
I am the real thing
Worth more you could ever, ever know
More better than the rarest of pure golds

But I am not a token
My Black is a something you can't own
I am not to be bought, to be owned, or sold
I am a dream lives on
conjured in the prayers of my ancestors
You are just itching to show me off
"Look, I got me one!"
A Black man

Black man
I am a Black man
Black man
You don't know how to act with a Black friend
I AM THE BLACK MAN
I am not a decoration
or a splash of color
or your goodwill
or your teacher

I will not teach you to be like me, speak like me
so you can be blissfully ignorant,
cashing in tokens,
moving through the world with a plagiarized pain you could
never understand

An Excerpt from *On the Last 400 Years,* a speech inspired by the riots of 2020 and the White anti-rioting rioters who get to insurrect in peace

Many are looking to us artists for something beautiful, something concrete, something to move us all forward with clear hearts and minds. I don't have a bunch of pretty words to espouse modern-day lynching and a fully enabled system of racism. I have no words to put out the fires. But if I am a bastion to some young man or woman walking in my footsteps, I offer this statement in fiery indignation . . .Black and Brown people and true allies across the color spectrum- be heard! And may God continue to allow fate to deal mightily with the hand of the oppressor.

FOR DEMBY

Today I am a Back man

Today I am a Black man
It cannot be undone
I die in the evening hours and then rise with the sun
I love this skin but I wish its conditions on no one
I am supposed to be ripped, I'm supposed to be well-hung
I'm supposed to not feel
I'm supposed to be strong

But today I am just strong enough to open my eyes
Maybe brush my teeth
Maybe tie my shoes
And maybe bite into an apple
Not much more I can do for you
My mind ain't as sharp as you want it to be for you
And I am not in the mood to be your strong Black man
I'm too jelly to break your back tonight babe
I'm too heavy to keep my head to the sky babe
I'm too underpaid to be your supply babe
And I'm slipknot away from being as solid as a rock

Babe- I cannot be your strong Black man today
I need help but don't make me out be a case
And in case I can't be that for you the next day or the next
In case I can't take a licking to bring home that check
In case I can't be your conqueror, king, or your perfect sex
In case I sleep a little bit longer than the rest
In case I can't laugh, cry or process my stress
Let me go down easy and don't stand in my way
. . . dark nights have had a way of dimming my days

And if I walk away from everything, then let it be a lesson
I'm not everything for everyone and that is the message
Today I am a Black man
However,
just strong enough to slip through the knot and fly into the arms of the moon.

31

I'm just thinking

overwhelmed at the way Demby suffered

by Austin Gore's hand

at any given time,

to rope off a Black man

was just easy

common

cost half a penny to kill a n++++r

and I'm just thinking

how ugly of a sentiment

how ghastly of a word

nigger

but among quick-witted Black folk

educated Black folk

Bible carrying, smooth talkin, soul bearing, African American Black folk

It's the commonest thing

I'm just thinking

it pisses me off

Call Me King

ngś
negus
niger
negra
nigger
niggra
negro
nigga- and every rationalization, every iteration, every
evolution, everything in between

If you cannot start from the beginning,
don't call me a thing.
too many distortions
too much caricature
too much energy to try and reclaim

I shouldn't have to search for myself in a slur.
You shouldn't have to justify poison to make it un-hurt
Black brother, I'm trying to change how we talk to each other.
        -like a human beings.
worthy of respect, at least
approached civilly
unmistakably hero
. . . brother
. . . god
. . . king

that's it, that's the vibes!
that's me, that's my energy!
call me King.

On Some Nxggah Shxt

I had been working there for eleven days when she fumbled. A coworker from the front-of-house saw me struggling with the garbage. She jokingly asked, "Do you need a man to do that for you?" We both laughed but I had that feeling that something was about to disrupt the peace. She rambled on, saying that she likes when she can joke without people getting offended. I knew then that she mistook my kindness for permission. It was coming. She gave an example of a time her friend got offended at one of her jokes. She continued, " He got all sensitive about it and I was like, 'niggah, it ain't that serious.' "

"Girl what?" I thought. It's tiring to have to still explain pejoratives in 2020. So I didn't. I walked away and focused on taking the trash out. I was pissed but I refrained from making a comment- disconcertingly passive. That feeling of "I should've said something" was swelling inside me. Yet, I stuffed it down- eyes bulging- as I persisted in taking out the trash.

Once inside the elevator and pressing the button, I could've sworn I saw Nat Turner in the corner holding up a sign that read, "IKYFL!" The longer I stood there on that elevator, the more ancestors started to appear. They were here to remind me. I stood jacked up by my apron, pressed against the elevator door as one of them said to me, "You best git yo' ass back in there and handle some shit!" I quickly exited the elevator, dusting off my improvisational skills as I headed for the building, on fire with the validity of my anger and the threat of my ancestors.

I arrived back on the crime scene- my ancestors piled behind me as if to say, "And you better tell her, too!" I asked for a moment with her. I began my recount, "Earlier, when we were talking, you playfully said the n word. I don't think it should be uttered. Not by you and not in the workplace. I don't even use it myself. It's not cool." She responded, " I didn't say that, I said 'niggah.' " She emphasized "ah" at the end of the pronunciation- like it was refreshing. I tilted my head, stretched my neck, and scrunched my brows. I thought of a less endearing expletive I wanted to call her and firmly responded, "There is no difference between n-i-g-g-e-r and n-i-g-g-a (h) and it shouldn't have come out your mouth, especially being surrounded by Black and Brown people-even if they choose to use it!" She said, "ok" in her nonchalant and slightly shaken way and continued working as I headed for the office to make my report.

I have written an open letter to her and her friends:

To the White girl who says "niggah" and the Black people who "gave her permission:"

This is NOT what Demby paid for, do you understand? As Dr. Angelou taught us, you cannot make this word beautiful. No one can use it safely. Might have meant something different before, but it doesn't mean that now and until we make a conscious return to original meanings, OPT OUT!

And this is not an argument on reclaimed things. You can reclaim a used G-string from a thrift store and that really doesn't make it a nice thing. Culture can be shifted! But I have little faith in a poor old G-string.

This is NOT-I repeat- this is NOT what Demby paid for in those chilly waters as men who considered it fairly cheap to kill a nigger, shot him to his death. Hearing that slur is like reading Demby getting shot all over again. Get your shit together where your lexicon has failed you . . . and don't let it be a next time.

Unreservedly,

Theodore Sylvester Holmes, III

BLACK LIBERATION

I Bet I'll Fly

I bet I'll rise
you can't take me anywhere I'm not made for
you'll see
freedom is my birthright
you snatched it from me

but I'll rise
I opened them doors for you
I and them ones of us you stole the land from, too
you're a no good thievin' alacabazaboo
you a stankin' ole polecat- everybody see you
but as sure as you keep on livin'
trouble gon' meet you and find you scheming
don't look for me,
I'll be somewhere getting the hell away from you
dreamin'
thrivin' like I'm 'posed to
yessuh! I bet I'll thrive

time getting' long now, ain't no use in trying to figure me out
this here is something that won't ever be understood
I bet you'll try 'cause this is a mystery, yea?
you'll keep proddin' and whippin',
killin' and lyin'
but a soul don't die
you may nail down my feet
rattle my mind
you may shoot me down in the river and strap boulders on my
sides-
but I bet you, I bet you
I'll fly

When you're born in chains
But this great God knows your name
You were always free

> I feel radical
> Suffused with an ancient joy
> My ancestor's tears

Tell them they can fly
Wake up and transcend the chains
Freedom has sent word

> The fourth of Ju-what?
> This is the day we get down
> We snatchin' our crowns

Letting Go (Cry Free)

I'm holding on to my faith
holding on to good friends
holding on to my sentiments
But sometimes it just depends
like when you keep tellin' 'em you matter- again and again
and they make a case for themselves, while they fight to cage
you in
So I'm letting go
Letting my words cry free!
I'm turning tables in the temple, bringing back the speech
blood wasn't merely spilled, it was poured in these streets
I pray they keep that same energy when it's time to bring the
heat
Take off their own pointy hats and burn their own white sheets
Strip these statues down to the white meat.

The New Activist

Resident costume lady-

"Pull your hat down, the homeboy look doesn't really work here."

And she yanked my hat down.

This was real

-a deliberate middle finger to my Blackness.

I witnessed this shrew flagrantly conspire with her colonizing forefathers

for my downfall.

It was a trick-

a spell to strike fear;

she wanted to micro-aggressively take my freedom,

but she couldn't have it.

Demanding submission,

but I wouldn't let her have it.

"It's my freedom and it's been paid for-

it is my people's song over me.

I'm not going to let you have it!"

Didn't she understand-

didn't someone read to her the implications?

She could not afford it-

"They cannot be played with

I am my ancestors' newness

They shed blood for me

They went hungry for me

They were burned, beat, and decorations for trees

Slashed, cuffed, and gassed because I was the dream

They walked miles across a bridge to bridge the gap for me

Did you not think they were with me?

I stand upon cocoa buttered shoulders

-Tan, Black, and Brown-

that stood their ground

Did you think I would forget?

There is a way from which we came and we will not turn back!

This be their bloodline.

This be the new activist.

Ain't no 'make the nigger mind' today-

ain't gonna be no pic-a-nig!

And I'm not going to be easy to deal with."

Truth is, I know she may not even regret she said it,

but maybe she'll think twice about testing a newly generated

activist.

And "no, I cannot pull my hat down- for lighting purposes.

The director has asked that my hat remain just above my face.

You'll have to see me shine all damn day."

The War of Intelligence ౦ ౦ ౦Sans Hypocrisy

Some years ago, just out of graduate school, I started to think, "How can we do this whole civil rights thing the effectively?" I wrote a blog post entitled, *"The War of Intelligence . . . Sans Hypocrisy."* I had so many ideas that I wanted to communicate. I was starting to reclaim my identity after some traumatic experiences and I was ready to join the freedom rides. My life was taking on a new meaning and so were my words, my art. I was frustrated because I didn't see the order in things and therefore, I couldn't see how we'd ever make it to a sound resolution. I grew irritated and nearly gave up the fight- a fight that had been making quite a difference before I jumped in it.

Looking back, I laugh at how serious I was at making people do what I said in my passive pseudo-Christian way. I was dead set on restoring order and good sense to the civil fight. I was also struggling with a Malcom/Martin complex. Those two leaders were different, but not unto discord and separation. They were as much one as they were of differing strategies. I worked overtime trying to represent one over the other. I wish someone had taught me that Dr. King also had righteous anger and that Brother Malcom also exhibited peace and that neither of those facts made any of their work less potent. Perhaps then, I wouldn't have forced a peaceful exterior while growing resentful from the anger I suppressed.

I wore myself out trying to lasso boisterous Black people while simultaneously making sure I disclaimed that not everyone is racist. Here I was using my precious energy trying to keep up appearances and I wasn't even using my mind. I was trapped in an assimilated mind. I was trained and rewarded constantly for being one of the "good ones." I was the quiet hypocrite; I was actually jealous of the people that had found their voice, their vocation, and their righteous expression of anger. I had a lot of feelings and a lot of heart, but the fight within me was yet to be discovered.

What I now understand an "intelligent civil fight" to be is one wherein we are grounded –aware of the present. I also understand it to be a war fought hand in hand with those who have come before us. And now that I am finished slapping people on the wrist for going with their gut, I can stick to the business of honoring them for fighting for me when I was ignorant and unwilling. Today, I can give my all to this fight. I can lock arms with the oppressed and cry freedom with my brothers and sisters. Our anger is valid. Our minds are valid. Our instincts are valid. Our peacefulness is valid. Our radicalness- on every front- is valid. Those things are all valid in this war and though I've questioned the concept of war, I believe that we are worth fighting for.

I stopped staving off transcendence and I allowed the revolution to awaken me and for my mind to evolve. It feels great to stop censoring myself for the sake of staying in agreement with others. Being agreeable isn't really one of those things I want to lead with on the battlefront. And if my non-Black associates and loved ones don't know, by now, the importance of this fight, their compliance is evident and it ain't on me to try and educate them. As for the ones who know, I am grateful.

It fills me with joy to finally exercise my expression of this inherent responsibility. I am honored to stand alongside so many people who are getting their hands messy and pushing towards a more free day. We all bring something special to the fight- and it's okay that it takes some of us a little longer to show up to the revolution. What matters is that we are here! With our very valid weapons and very valid and varying tactics. I fight with my words, my stories, and my art. I find the sages in history and I keep their message close to my heart. I tell my truth in spite of oppressive norms. I keep hope alive. I start trouble. And as that is such, there is hope for me yet. Fight on good people. Fight for the cause of Black Liberation!

SOLIDARITY

Doris

she boarded the bus
bright as day
sweet like a kiss
infectious smile
dipping between languages
-for her friend and for the driver
I remembered her voice-
  how it made me feel
and her eyes,
dancing above her face mask
she fed me before
Doris

I called out to her
"did you used to work at the cantina?"
"Yes, I did!"
"I remember you, your voice
you always use to feed me."
"Ahh yes, Papi! How are you?"
she reaches her hand out to squeeze mine
her *marron* to my brown
her journey tied to mine
her strength upholding me
  I had nearly wilted
except she lay hold me
fixed me in the light
filled my plate again

A Dedication in Solidarity

I dedicate this poem to Black and Brown people shuffling along. Struggling to feel worthy-to feel seen against the American flag and not pressed into its creases . . . where the red turns into white. You are there. Folded into the stars. You know who you are. Black and Indigenous People of Color.

I dedicate this to all people. People who let nature be wide and big. A space that is enough for all of us to live. This is for my White neighbors who say hello without me always having to initiate. This is for the salesperson that lets me shop in peace. This is for the bike repair shop that always treats me like the rest of the somebodies. And for the radical friends that walk by our sides. There you all are striving to make this land more free.

I dedicate this to my ancestors. I am your possibility. Thank you for finding a way to survive. Thank you for sending me back here when I wanted to die. Thank you reminding me time after time. And thank you for your whispers.

I dedicate this to the Great Artist, I am undone with gratitude and overwhelming joy that we get to exist in your BELOVEDNESS-and that, because you wanted it so. You wanted us here.

We are your calligraphy-all peoples gathered wholly for the holiness of solidarity.

Your unmistakable imprint-
lasting,
indelible.

Big Brother

"Martín, can you drop me some fries and tenders?"
"I got you buddy."
I had done my shift and a half.
I was hungry-
rushing to catch the bus.
it was too chilly to wait for another hour.

I ran to clock out
before anyone asked me to do anything else
and he gave me my food.
"Thanks brother! You work tomorrow?"
"No, I work Thursday though."
"Cool, I'll see you then."
"Take care buddy."

I hoped I hadn't missed the bus.
The stop seemed miles away-
my feet were hurting.
I had an attitude and an angry belly.
The bus was late.
"I might as well eat."
I opened bag with my fries and tenders,
the container read, "Brother Teddy"
I mattered.

I cried when he stopped working there.
I knew he covered me in more ways than food.
He never got upset when I asked, "Papi, what does this
mean?"
I knew he knew the grief of a hardworking Brown man living
in America.
I know that he will always wish me well.
He had vowed to be my brother.

White Friends

Thank you for being a friend

and keeping that the focus

no strange permissions

no cultural inappropriateness

just good ole carrying on

like friends do

I appreciate that you don't feel

. . . anxious

to say ignorant stuff

like references to Tupac

or afros

or chicken

or presidents

or soul food

it means a lot

-to be befriended in a way that neither of us have to perform

or prove my Blackness

BLACK HUMANITY

For Ones Who Have Tried to Unmake Themselves

it happened. slowly but certainly, it happened. i wanted to un-be myself. i saw this man with a gorgeous mane and wished it was mine. i wished for his hairline. a bit more melanin. a bit more height. more muscle, more appeal. new clothes, new pose, bowed legs. something to make me a standout, a groundbreaking black man. then… i looked down at my loose skin. my fat ear lobes. skim hairline. thick thighs hugging and touching-a pillar beneath my muffin top. and i climbed to the mountaintop of my sex, the love i give. my holy brown. and somehow I start to smile where I planned to unmake myself.

Retta

kneeling among the debris
searching for pieces, toiling to bring it all together
hoping to find life among the ashes
some brute has come and fought you for your gladness
what has undone the life you imagined?
you, young mother are a diamond
you appear strikingly beautiful as you grope among the ashes
overwhelmed by the aftermath

you have started over more times than you can bear to think
tucking away your dreams more solemnly each time
you have tried to stand up and remember yourself
but somehow life has found you here on your knees
in the ashes of the aftermath
singing your somber song, trying to move your family along
      it hurts to be here
but you young mother are a diamond
and though this heaviness befalls you,
you appear strikingly beautiful as you kneel,
groping among the ashes
overwhelmed by the aftermath

many of your kind are dying. I pray you don't go and die too.
Imagine a tomorrow. adorn your feet. revere your frame- your
body has been good to you. stand tall, towering. remember
yourself. what is your name? un-tuck your dreams and let
them fly free!

because you young mother, are a diamond
and though this heaviness befalls you-
appearing quite tragic-
and though some strange thing has devoured your hope of
ever getting past this
you appear strikingly beautiful
      as you rise from among the ashes,
        shimmering.

Love's Knot ... inspired by Black Love

I have decided to unravel,
Give my whole self irreversible exposure
... to communion
To hold your hands
To match your fingertips down to my fingerprints

I have never done this for anyone,
but for you, I will unravel
For an extended stay in your embrace
I will be present
As God is my witness, you can know my deepest secrets
Know my joy.
Know my fears.
Share my favorite chap stick ...
We stick together like a pretty pack of post-its-
Holding on

And oh my, I never thought I'd see the day I'd do this,
But I am unraveling myself for you.
I lay my hand upon your hand and-
it's like a double layer cake and God-
Well, God is our chocolate *ganache*.
We are a union standing on the Rock
And nothing will blot out this happy spot
          the fire will blaze
          the ruthless will plunder
But God cannot be expended
God will not be bent
God is the invincible lock in our thread

We've made our bid and invested everything we've got
We have unraveled ourselves
And we take hold of Love's lot
With joy we submit to this tying of God's knot

Oh How She Danced

This one girl
This girl made me excited to see!
Thankful to the heavens for the function of vision,
Because oh how she danced

She was striking, towering above me
Maybe it was her beauty
Maybe it was how she released me
Made me feel like I can love somebody and be loved

Had this one particular song playing in my head-
Had it on repeat!
And this sweet dream,
God made her
God wrote the moments that I spent with her
She was so pure
I wanted to give her all of the me's in my pocket
It was how she danced

I don't understand how somebody can be walking and dancing
at the same time-
She did!
How somebody can be talking and dancing and the same time-
She did!
Laughing and dancing,
Gazing and dancing,
Breathing and dancing all at the same damn time!
How queer and daring to think that she could be mine
That she'd be the one exception in my lifetime
To love a woman aloud, a darling possibility
It was how she danced

For Persons in the Beautiful Struggle

This morning, I woke up thinking of ways I could pay my rent
Pondering failed computer updates and high interest rates
And I thought about the different ways I could prepare the
same meal again
I thought about how my career, as I've known it, is changing
But I- most unrelentingly- have vowed to dream
even if I have to eat the same old thing for a little while

Found my friend in a hash tag
I've been sorting through ideas about death
How we mourn our fathers, heroes, and friends
Things are so uncomfortable right now
I'm tense, I'm tired, and it's slightly hard to smile
        . . . hard times

I thought about how I can't find my groove
Sitting opposite creativity in a dreary sort of mood
And no matter how much I grow, regardless to how much I
bloom- somebody is a few dollars ahead of me
Lecturing me
Judging me for not having
Disregarding who I am
Reducing me to what I do

But no man is exempt from a few days of troubles
You can get it now or a little ways down the road
So I'm enduring like a gent
Me and all my 16¢
'Cause I know for a fact it won't always be like this
And ain't nobody about to make me feel like the dusty whatnot
in the corner

Some pockets of society teach us to forget that we are everyday people
But whether your computer cord is frayed or if you're down in the rubble
Whether you're sick, between jobs, or knee-deep in trouble
This poem is quite literally for all my people in the struggle

A change is coming.

Remember Your Father's Hands

Remember your father's hands
And disregard the heartbreak
Remember his time in the burning sun and his hands gone raw
Because he needed to take care of his family
He could've walked away
But then you would've had a different kind of pain

So remember his jokes
His efforts to be playful on a Saturday morning
Table magic
Coin tricks
And his limp
Subtle through the years
How he leaned when he stood
How he carried in the wood-
Remember the fires
That satiating smell of smoke
Toasty corners of the house and all of us gathered around
eating butterscotch candies
Excited for tomorrow's dinner request he'd submitted to
mama
Biscuits, salmon patties, sausage, and syrup

Remember his head
Crowned with sweat
How he steeped the room in prayer and fasted breath
Gripping your hand tightly
He prayed like heaven would come down
Remember his frown-
he was well-frowned
It wasn't always unpleasant
Understand his complexities
The demand for his time left him inundated with pressure
Often contemplating and scratching his head
Remember that he is a man

The List

There is a list sitting in the back of your head right
now. Written on it are things from yesterday that made you
feel unworthy. You had no idea that you wrote it. You tote it
around, sleep with it, and wake up with your value in question.
You must put it on the table . . . and part ways with it.

text messages from which you never received a reply
you smiled but the cashier rolled their eyes
A bill that slid you back six dollars
An offensively empty refrigerator that made you want to holler
The advice you got and never asked for to begin
Social media flexes from your well-to-do "friends"
A "Hello" from the perfect stranger
        -and the missed connection
The long gone relationship that crossed your thoughts again
hair in the food, car on "e", and you feel like you can't win
The walk to the coin machine as your store crush stared on
The incoming calls from that debt collector who will not leave
you alone- the list goes on

but you have to give it up
. . . and light it on fire
Watch it burn.
pray.
For only God and Her kind thoughts can baptize the stench
away
Let yourself be saved.
dunked.
purged underwater.
flinching
-until the monster it made you is uncreated
        until what remains of the list has faded
Until, at last, you come to good sense
and God pulls you back to safety. . . stillness

You might wonder if something is missing...but sometimes it's
good to forget.

BLACK TRADITIONS

We inspire me. I am inspired by our traditions and our values. I am captivated by our qualities and fortified by our community. I am strengthened by the way we live-boldly, undeterred. I like the way we talk, walk, dance, love, and lift the vibes. I like how we say hello and goodbye. I like the way we cover each other; the men and women who are on post watching over us. Sometimes it's just a nod and sometimes it's just a "Hey Baby!" Either way it's village. I like the things that make us laugh for eons. I like the way we remember. I like how we pray. I like the unspoken traditions and unanimous decisions. The way we love to eat. The way we love cocoa butter and Shea butter and oils, and grease. Every moment and with every fiber of my being, I am beyond grateful for our things. There could never be enough books about us. There is a lot that's good about us! Despite things that may disappoint, I'm going to keep vibrating higher for us. I am proud to be a Black man.

Things We Heard, Things We Will Say

I'm finda hit the hay
We got church in the morning
and we gotta swang by at ya cousins
sit that sawsheh in the in the frigerator to thaw

Go get me a switch off that tree
I told y'all bout cutting up in the store
You thought I forgot
I'm finda tear y'all behind up

who put this food in the trash
y'all know that go in with the dog food
and somebody been playin over this chicken
I don't buy food for y'all to waste

Come hand me this remote
what the devil you was in there doing
if you can "huh?" you can hear
put it on my show

hush that fuss or imma give you something to holler bout
acting like somebody done killed you
ain't near bout taught you like I could've
don't let that schoolhouse have to call me for nothing else

what you doing scared
you must've been doing something you ain't had no business
that's just what you get
I told you to sit down somewhere

y'all acting like yall ain't never been nowhere
don't get to Ma house acting like y'all ain't ate neither
get out from up under him like that
go somewhere and get out grown folks business

you can sit there sullen if you want to-
gone be sittin there all night 'til you finish it
Y'all better speak when you walk in this house
Stay in or out and keep my do' closed. . . letting flies in my house

60

Bonnets

Bonnets are a Black tradition

they favor your edges

they save you from split ends

. . . they run when you call them

Hairline (Inheritance)

high up on the right
scooched back on the sides
I've wondered sometimes
if I should just let it go
grows so fast-and not in the places that I want
I want Sampson locs
I want freeform tree trunks
but my stuff is frizzy
some parts scruffy, some parts soft
I've been so mad, I've cut it all off
I want that hairline barbers lust for
I want that strong black wavy tide
I pray each and every follicle can be revived
I want the barber to make me myself again-it's tradition

But every time they hand me the mirror
I see . . . my grandfather
long gone
left me without so much as a fun memory
but in these passing moments, I hear him speak
"Grandson, I could not give you much in life.
time lay hold of me, but I do have. . .
this kinked and curly crown-
It is mine and yours and ours, though imperfectly underlined."

high up on the right
scooched back on the sides
an inheritance

family reunion

dark green shirts. fruit punch and cream sodas. lake jackson.
too scared to go too far into the woods. pictures with the
elders. so much macaroni salad. so much meat on the grill.
i'm just trying to find the tater chips and pound cake but auntie
got me eating these green beans. folks dancing to blues.
watching for grandma's reaction to see if she approves. ya
cousin's friend is cute. wait- somebody fixin' to fight. never
mind, deacon daddy and uncle old school will get it back right.
how is he my uncle anyway?
"where y'all going?"
"we finda run to the sto' "
"y'all come sang us a song before y'all go"
I wish my parents let me spend the night with somebody.
posing on cars that ain't yours. lost in a sea of people that IS
yours.
safely forgotten.
among blood.
under the evening sun
watching your tipsy uncles go off. . . like this a soul train.
wishing you would've been brave enough to venture off. now
you ain't got time. cause daddy said go crank up the van. last
pictures before we take it in.
"y'all hurrup and wrap up some plates before flies get to em"
this has been a beautiful day- cuz low key trying to keep the
party going. but y'all know we got church in the morning!

DNA

This morning, I felt like my father as I placed my raggedy handkerchief back into my pocket. I saw a long line of men saying hello to me as I moved in and out of their rhythm- a lineage of working men. Muscle memory. DNA.

The Nod

It happens in an instant

an intimate fortification of the Black male bond

some are too distracted to catch it

some are too macho to offer it

but when it happens, young boys fly

and old men become immortal

and when words are exchanged,

it is like opening up a portal

opening up a healing

initiation

the nod

BLACK REALITIES

An Urgent Matter

Careful these days,
Before you run up on one.
You'll think you got a friend 'til you find yourself hung
. . . in the noose of their illusion.
Three years into a friendship and you got the wrong Susan
She pulls you in and she calls you Black Son
Goes blabbing to her friends, "I got me one"
But the race war stirs and she gets horny for destruction
The capital is stormed in a blatant insurrection
They speed in big trucks, with confederate erections
Even their Black friends and their kin got to bow to the
cataclysmic confusion
Be careful that you don't end up with a colonialist contusion

Careful, be vigilant and keep your eyes to the sun
Pay attention to the humble, they the ones you can trust
Not the gun-toting Christians singing the national anthem
Not the colorblind crusaders
Not the lecturing ones who like proving a point
        It's all a part of the fabric of assimilation
Trust the humble ones
Who walk quietly beside you through storms
Not so God can get the glory- not for brownie points
But because love and appreciation...
Just love and appreciation

Trust the humble
Them who think before they talk
Them who cover you when the world is on fire
Who help you start fires when the world is dark
Who help you start fires when the world is warped
Them who don't talk down to you
Them who don't get off on saving Black people
Them who don't mind raising families right next to you
Them who get loud when it counts and won't shut up until
justice is won
Trust the humble ones

Who walk beside you through storms and good weather
And that, just because . . .

But stay vigilant
Even though there are ones you can trust
Be rooted like a tree, lest you be strung on one

Magical White People

there is more than magical white people

there is more than exceptional black people doing what is only
expected of white people:

more than exceptional sidekicks

more than well spoken and brainy phenomena

more than surprisingly able black folks.

BUT WE ARE MORE THAN SUPRISING

sensational is the norm

so DO NOT WRITE ME OUTSIDE OF WHERE THE
MAGIC HAPPENS

we magic, too- I know you heard about us

I have lived it and I can prove it-

There is more to us!

But every time I turn on the tv.... goddam

The Hunted

inspired by Ahmaud and men they call Black .

Called my momma
love her so
talked our talk
talked some mo'
she asked what I was doing
"Headed to the sto' . . ."
Said I was biking like usual
It changed her tone
she begged me to get home
before the street lights come on

Called my momma
Love her so
she gets nervous when I say
"I'm walking out the do' . . ."
she sees me as her son
but she sees so much more
A Black man in America
Hunted like a boar

There Has Been A Lynching

I wanted to record this in a field, no ceilings
I wanted to call my friend with the good camera
Wanted to copyright this and make it official
To make official my sentiments as I heaved and hurled them to
the sky
Make my neighbors peep through their blinds
As I confront the colonizers spirit
For the mess he left behind

So I wrote some notes on how it was and still is living as a
Black man, bleeding as a Black man, anxious like a Black man,
and dying in America

I cannot look at castile soap the same
My mind goes back to the day Philando was HANGED
I was sick with worry
Buried in sadness
I could not move
I could not manage
I could not breathe when they pinned down Eric
Lynched in plain sight to strike fear in the village
And they pillaged
Up and down these roads
In and out these homes
Sniffing out Black Souls that might be a threat.
Do you know how it feels to live as black persons with these
images in your head,
to try and keep your spirit high with this shit inside your
chest?
Sick with worry
Steeped, STEEPED in sadness

Because Sean
Because Betty
Because Alton
Because Eric

Because Sandra
And Breonna
And Atatianna
And every Black sacrifice made on the altar of fear and
supremacy
In the name of white pointy hats
In the name of dear old flag
In the name of whose forefathers?
    -not mine

THERE HAS BEEN A LYNCHING
Blacks and Browns must die

I remember being pulled over for the first time
A cold feeling of death gripped my spine
I THOUGHT HE WAS GOING TO KILL ME
He approached from my passenger side and asked where was
the gun
He said his system showed that I had a registered gun
I said, "My name is Theodore Sylvester Holmes the 3rd and to
my knowledge I am the only one"
He said once more, "so where's the gun?"
I THOUGHT HE WAS GOING TO KILL ME
After all that he said he wanted to tell me about my dead
headlight
I didn't even want to drive again
I didn't want a car

Last year I got into an accident right outside my house
I was relieved
Just one less way for them to threaten me
One less was to seem threatening
Everyone kept saying "when you gonna get a car"
But I was focused on staying alive
And it really don't matter if you in a car
You could be on your own street or out on your porch
You could be out with your mom
Or out for a jog

And oh God, Ahmaud

I WANTED TO DIE

I floated through the store in a strange state of mind
Stricken with despondency
A sudden fury of the bad feeling
I thought maybe it was empathy
Maybe I just need a cool drink
I left the store but I COULD NOT SHAKE THE FEELING
Bleak
I sped off on my bike Ahmaud
I reached the corner Ahmaud
Nina Simone playing in my ear
Yea mama, IT"S SO GODDAMNED HARD . . . to live
And stopped on that corner Ahmaud
I reached inside Ahmaud
And I pulled us up Ahmaud
And WE CRIED WITH YOU
Black men and women are crying with you
They running too
And Ahmaud I SCREAMED
Cause THERE HAS BEEN A LYNCHING

May all that's good and right
Break the chain in our society
May the souls of black folk
Return mightily
May we run with the sun until our work is done
May we run with the sun until our work is done
Start a righteous war
And run with the sun

And now for _____

73

But Hope

Some days, all I can hear is the sound of my own heartbeat
like my heart is pushing through my ear drums
pressure like underwater
pressure like underwater
pressure is underwater and I cannot swim
pressurized conscience
my conscience caves in

I close my eyes and I try to leave it all behind
I thought I had died but that turned out to be a lie

I'm still here and I just cannot believe it
I meant to be gone-
in an instant.
fixed beneath the chilly shores

I tried to die
nearly impossible when hope wells up inside
where did it come from?
inflating me and yanking me up from the ice bath
where did it come from?
rising high, drowning out the sullen requiem
hope-
          drumming up a war in my name
hope-
          pounding in my chest
hope is bringing me back again

I lost my mind that night-
fading under icy waters
life slipping from this body
and I didn't know if I wanted to return
          -but hope.

FORERUNNER

Grandmother's Fire

I built a ring of fire
Inside of it I cried
Inhaled all of the flames
And made a future for my children

Lord!
they tied me up, hung me up
but I'm coming down alive
Out of this life and into the next
they won't kill me a second time,
for I live on in my children

oh the mighty price I paid
that my children may fly
that emblems made from torches blazed
should light their way to guide

I, beholding my fate,
in the most harrowing of days
thought of you-
and I built a ring of fire.

Ancestry Project

The following poems and journal entries are from an ancestry project that I was able to take part in at my Alma Mater. For a summer, we struggled to get to the truth. We were stressed, we hit walls, and we had breakthroughs. I discovered that we all just wanted so badly to know ourselves and from whence we came.

5/21/10

the veil is lifting
today I will see my face
God what is my name

6/01/10

There is a hidden pride in what and who we are. It is enhanced when we listen to each other speak.

6/04/10

You've been invisible
you there
you have hidden your face from me
you there, on my face
Did you think I'd be afraid of where I found you
did you think I'd wash you off like dirt

you there
you've been invisible
you there, springing through my pores
emerging, leaking- bitter, salty
I have tasted your tears

You there
please don't hide my self from me

you there, nestled quietly under my skin
you've been invisible
but I think you ought to know, I'll carry you proudly
you there, in that tan skin
that cream skin
that yellow, black, that red skin
that's MY skin
I'm not afraid to remember you
I won't wash you off
I'm not ruined-I still want you
You there
you've been invisible

6/09/10

They all have secrets
I have all of the questions
I dig for answers

6/12/10

If you want to know
what it is that I'm feeling
you can check my pulse

6/17/10

Journal Entry

The tension has risen and continues to peak in our ancestry curriculum. It may be due to the heat, monotonous classroom settings, student-professor issues, small breaks, and hunger. Then again, it may simply be our yearning to get to the finish point . . . to know the outcomes. The expedition is tedious! Ancestors can you meet us halfway?

6/30/10

Journal Entry

I am being traced to East and Sub-Saharan Africa with a "move" traced to Cameroon and Benin. Ok!??

7/1/10

I think I know me
I'm Cameroon and Benin
Reach out and touch me

open document
the language speaking people
it makes perfect sense

skilled metal workers
five hundred plus languages
I love my people

7/4/ 10

I found some more names
I wish they would just talk to me
Am I listening?

7/05/10
Family is a trip
The art of devouring truth
Someone has to talk

7/13/10

Rounding off AP
What has this journey rendered?
We must look deeper

With the Light On (for Ms. Cicely)

I am folding
I want to go inside myself . . . to say goodbye
my heart swells with utmost thank you's
my mind is swamped with an onslaught of who knew's
who knew that you were saying goodbye these last few years
gracing the red carpets
dazzling, fierce
walking amongst your children
they stand on a platform you paved
a way you made in the darkest of your days
clear and bright
lighting the way for a million and one somebodys to be the one
body that dares to dream
urging us to stop half lighting our dreams
and set fire to this field of candles
dancing under the night we shine bright for this time we live in
a trill so ripe with possibility

and I am folding
I want to go inside myself. . .to say goodbye
that is where you have touched
that is where the memory of your time resides
in my inmost being

I want to turn off the lights
seal the blinds
close every door and be near the light that you left on for me
you left the light on for me
I was a wounded storyteller, journeying along some
troublesome road
and that you would know I was coming after you was nothing
short of a mystery
I could only have wished to be on a stage with you
holding hands in the name of literature
to behold you
a living well of goodness from which we all wanted a drink

every young mans grandmother
every young woman's dream
shepherding daring nightingale
our charming queen

Alas I did not greet you here
and that would've been an unfortunate thing-
except, I journeyed deep inside me
and there, ahead of some troublesome road you stood
beckoning
with the light on
thank you

Don't Cover the Wounds

Don't. Cover. The wounds.
For from them comes a tune about how you made it through
      the darkness.
You were given a yoke
      -harnessed.
You fought when no one was looking,
your fight proves honest.
And now we raise a toast for the champions among us.

This I tell you, men and women like you are one in a few.
People like you have no proving to do-
the proof is in your story.
A long and arduous journey marked by blood and
      hallowed footprints.
We traced them to when you chose persistence.
We uncovered so many fears, unaware that you had them.
We learned great fire fell and you ran past it.
We raise our glass, for there are real champions in our midst.

Your survival on this journey is what is lighting our lanterns-
It will be our honor to study your patterns.
And while I have stammered to let yes be my answer,
you chose "yes" over comfort and that is why I am able to
stand here.
A mere fan among millions in the generations
who look upon you lovingly,
who know and understand that-
we are staring into the eyes of champions

Will to Live

There are days when I thought of dying
Wanting it to be over
Wanting a real reason to roll over-
In the morning
And then I think of my people
The fight
The love
Those shining down from above
And who walk among us
They give me so much hope I believe I can go on
A tad more
Pushing through that glass door to the new day
I've thought-only thought- of dying
Bar my celestial rescue,
By which my ancestors urged me to seize the day

It was there
Daylight in the eyes of black children
The elders
The artists and all those called misfits
Loud and angry
Sad and bemoaned
Alone
But not quite alone
An anthem
An answer
Black people -my Black people-are a beautiful reason to live
I got the Will to live

JUBA

I discovered an inherent joy in writing about Black people . . .
all of us- a deep joy. It is like placing my hands on organ keys
and witnessing the sound- leaping, thunderously, from my
computer screen. Singing back to me . . . from the worlds in
my fingertips. Rich, sweet, and dearly Black.

wonderful ME!

Ha! What joy besieges me
Started from the womb of the Most High
Came crashing down to my lowest like a comet in the dark
night
And now I'm here
Awake
And I survived the breaking
I survived the burning
a form-fitting journey for a Phoenix
I rise from the ash again and again
In constant display of celebration

I'm celebrating Christ-likeness
Image-bearing Brown man
Brawn and Beauty
Crowned with the light of the sun
Hand-spun, fearfully
Wonderful me, wonderful me!

Black People Are Not Monoliths

Black People are not monoliths
we be Mama and God too
Holy people, holy wombs
a universe inside

Stretched wide across nations
Afro-Latinx, Afro-indigenous, Afro-Asian
Our shades are all encapsulating

Albinism for the algorithm-
by which we understand the expanse of the Creator's palette
Vitiligo and birth marked souls
for by which we have deepened what it is to be Black

Two-spirited gems and gents and femmes
who brought the rainbow back
churched, mosqued, and templed
Big, thin, and dimpled
long crowns, locked crowns, bald glory
we are an allegory of sacredness
a Holy people, holy wombs

There is a universe inside
each of us staring down this broad stretch of table
some with ten fingers, two hands, two arms, legs, and ten toes
and some without
some quite endowed
some disabled. . .we are yet a staple
an undying tradition of possibility whirling and welling up
from the tops of our heads to the soles of our feet

Oh God
God is to be praised for His work
and for Her Excellence
Who has flattened the myth that we are beneath God's very
benevolence
we are evergreens
a complete and total mystery

We are not monoliths
we be Mama and God too
Holy people, holy wombs
a universe inside

Cleo

Sweet Geechee Daughter
Brown like sugar be, too sweet
Your spirit with me

Melanin

when I feel the sun against my skin

    -the loud rays against my hue-

i'm so glad i'm not its enemy.

i feel crowned, recharged, empowered.

made fluorescent in the night of my skin's glow

    . . . my whole soul aglow

My Sweet Black

My hair, my ash

My lips, my smack

My blends-

My friends I love my Black

I cannot apologize for that

That caramel pecan is what makes my sweet Black

My sweet back, sweet legs, hands

Sweet Black

I got love for my swirly pedigree

My Norway, my UK, my Afghanistan sweet

But my Black is the most controversial part of me

To some, I seem like poison, tragically bitter

Yet somehow, I've been found way deep down

     -and things just got sweeter

My song got deeper

Path got steeper and there I got to meet Her

My Africa, **My Sweet Black**